My Birthmark & ME!

Couragetoclimb.co.uk

copyright©2023 JazieaFarag

All rights reserved.

For my three beautiful children, Bella, Elijah, and Órlaith, who inspire me every day with their imagination and endless questions. Ben, my partner in crime and chief grammar checker, and my Mum, Dad, and little sister Layla, for always giving me the confidence to believe I can do anything.

I love you all.

I have a **MAGICAL BIRTHMARK.**

It can be what I want it to be.

Just close your eyes.

Count 1, 2, 3...

... and come on this journey with me.

My birthmark is ...

LIONS eating,

at a picnic on the beach.

My birthmark is...

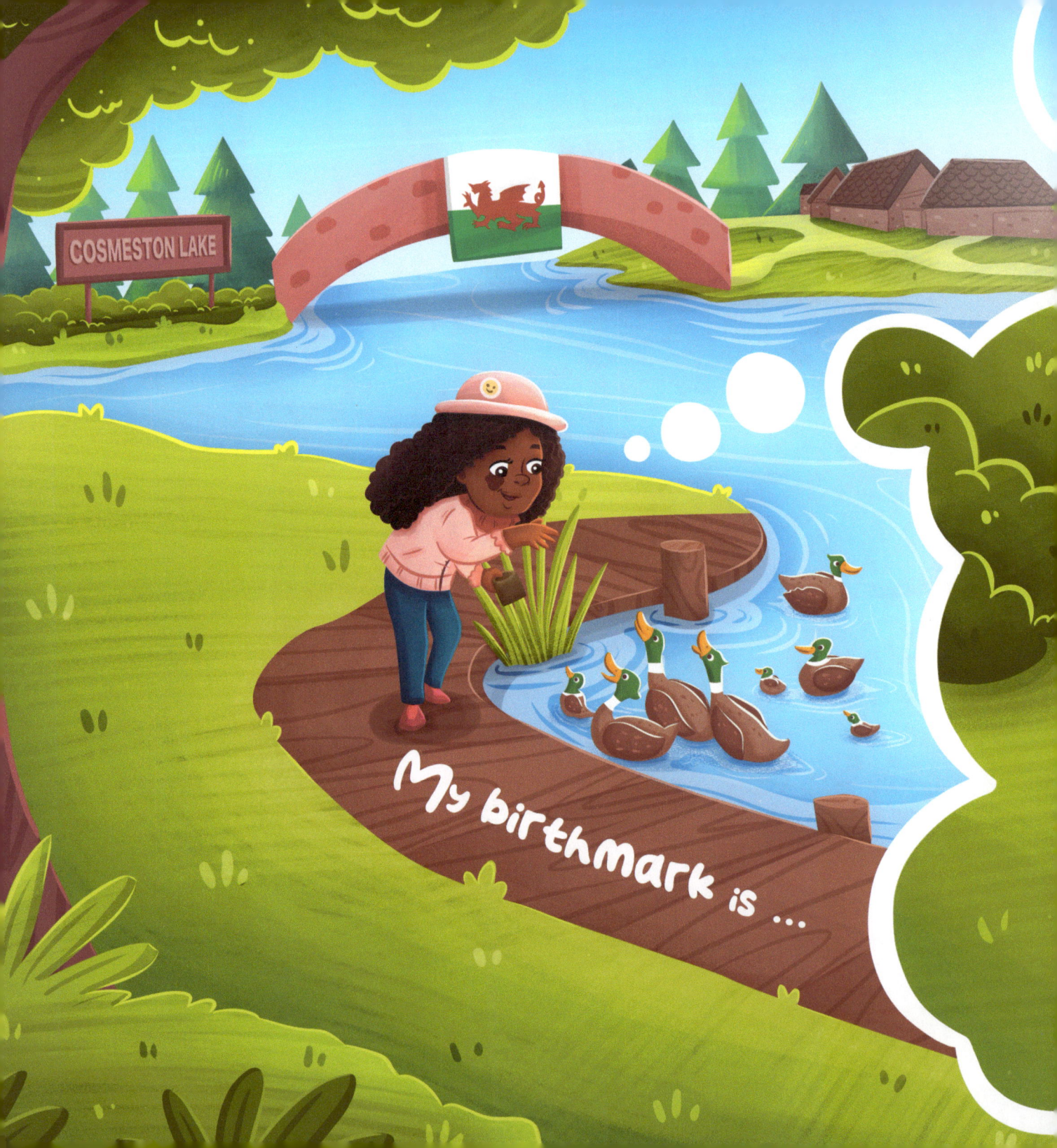

CROCODILES planting, in the garden on their knees.

About the Author

Jaziea Farag has always had a passion for reading, but as a child felt that children like her were underrepresented as positive protagonists. As an Advisory Teacher and Education Consultant she understands the power that books have, to really connect with children and has always advocated for books with a positive message.

As a mother to three curious creators with vivid imaginations, she is never too far away from a journey through the jungle, a trip to Mars or a hike through the Jurassic era.

Being born with a magical birthmark on her face, Jaziea took some time to learn to embrace and eventually love her unique feature!

She is hoping that this book will help children to appreciate their differences, love themselves and realise how amazing it is to be them.

www.ingramcontent.com/pod-product-compliance
Lightning Source LLC
Chambersburg PA
CBHW042127040426
42450CB00002B/106